HowExpert

CW00766129

How To ____
Insects

Your Step By Step Guide
To Drawing Insects

HowExpert with
Stefani Neumann

Copyright HowExpert™
www.HowExpert.com

**For more tips related to this topic,
visit HowExpert.com/insects.**

Recommended Resources

- HowExpert.com – Quick 'How To' Guides on All Topics from A to Z by Everyday Experts.
- HowExpert.com/free – Free HowExpert Email Newsletter.
- HowExpert.com/books – HowExpert Books
- HowExpert.com/courses – HowExpert Courses
- HowExpert.com/clothing – HowExpert Clothing
- HowExpert.com/membership – HowExpert Membership Site
- HowExpert.com/affiliates – HowExpert Affiliate Program
- HowExpert.com/writers – Write About Your #1 Passion/Knowledge/Expertise & Become a HowExpert Author.
- HowExpert.com/resources – Additional HowExpert Recommended Resources
- YouTube.com/HowExpert – Subscribe to HowExpert YouTube.
- Instagram.com/HowExpert – Follow HowExpert on Instagram.
- Facebook.com/HowExpert – Follow HowExpert on Facebook.

Table of Contents

Introduction

Have you ever found yourself in your yard on a mild summer evening and listen to all the sounds around you? You can hear buzzing, chirping, fluttering and scrambling in the air and the ground. Bugs, insects and creepy crawlers are everywhere, scuttling around and serving their purpose in the bug world. Of course, we will always delight in the obvious beauties like the butterfly or the dragonfly. That is why I included them in our drawing book. They are my favorite, because their wings display an array of stunning colors or are a piece of unparalleled translucent beauty. The ladybug and the green grasshopper are delightful fellows to observe and the spider, though creepy at times, is always a fascinating subject to study. Her appearance often gives us the creeps, and some people suffer from the fear of spiders, but books like "Charlotte's Web" have done a lot to draw attention to the beautiful art a spider creates. In fact, the spiders are the artists of the bug world. They create stunning compositions of symmetry and delicacy with their spider web design. If you go outside on an early September morning, search your yard for the magnificent webs that are spun at night.

But the world of bugs does definitely have its nasty and creepy side. It is just fair that I included my absolute least favorite bug in this book as well. That would be the pincher bug. The sight of it makes me shiver and it is one nasty little fellow. However, if we are speaking of pinchers, there is also the scorpion that is quite a threat to the bug world. Its big claws and stinging tail warn us that this is not somebody to mess with. Speaking of, the praying mantis is another formidable predator that is harmless to humans, but watch out bug world. She is the lion king of the insect world and dominates the food chain among the grass, flowers and dirt. She even bites the head of her own kind.

Most insects do leave humans alone and many flying creatures serve the purpose of pollinating our plants and flowers, thus sustaining life and nourishment for the human race and beyond. A fun guest around the garden is a bee. Lovely bees give us honey and we like them for that, even though they can sting. For some reason we forgive them for the pinch, because they die if they sting us. We view its likeness, the wasp in an entire different light. The wasp is an aggressor and known to attack humans, so we vote no for the wasp and yes for the bee. I included both in our book, as their differences are subtle, but yet distinguished when drawing either one of them.

Then of course, we have the janitors of the bug world. Some creepers are just there to clean up. Well, the pincher bug is probably one of the biggest contributors to a clean environment. It just eats about anything, dead or alive and therefore keeps the dirt world clean. The ant is another useful scavenger to have around the yard. It works constantly and picks up dead pieces of wings or legs and rotten berries and fruit. However, every once in awhile, the ant errs its way into our pantry and it is not a welcomed visitor over there.

The winners for the downright creepiest bugs are the centipede and the cockroach. Yuck on all levels, but I felt that they also have a right to be studied and drawn. After all, creepy crawlers have a certain kind of charm. Okay, I am going to correct myself. The, for me at least, nastiest ever bug is the potato bug. I tried to include it in the book, but I found that I could not bring myself to draw it. It is one big, nasty, slimy critter.

In addition, we have the pesky buggers like the housefly and the mosquito. Typically, we also feel not a lot of warm feelings towards these flying insects, but they are a common guest in or house and it does not hurt for us to take a closer look at their physique. We may be able to appreciate the beauty of their wings or limbs. Flies actually have this beautiful iridescent green color, however their shady posture make them unappetizing to look at. The mosquito also has a very slouched physique and is not a proud bug for sure. It also happens to drive us crazy with its whining. Geez.

If we stay out past the sunset, we see the night crawlers emerge. One kind, the not so liked, very unwelcome kind of bug in every garden is the snail. It slithers out at night and snacks on about any flower, bush or berry it can find and it is doing a lot of damage in the process. One does not know what to think of snails, as they have a fascinating beauty within their shell, but oh boy, can they destroy a garden. The other, much more beautiful night visitor is the moth. Its wings are fabulous and you are lucky if you catch a peek of this magnificent creature. Of course, your nighttime browsing will be accompanied by the romantic chirping of the lonely grasshopper.

Naturally, bugs do not exist in a vacuum, so some of our drawings include sketches of their environment as well. But truly, the world of bugs includes the world of flowers, soil and sky. They all exist in symbiosis with each other, so if you are daring, add flowers and rocks to your drawing. Well, we may just have to create another book that deals with drawing flowers.

No matter which insect you gravitate to, bugs are fun and quite interesting in their design and body shape. Next time you swat at a pesky critter, take the time to study its form, legs and wings and you may see beauty hidden away.

Chapter 1: The Art of Drawing

Drawing is a fundamental skill for all the art forms. If you can draw, you can take your images to an entire new level by adding paint, watercolors or computer induced graphics. However, at the base of all art forms lays the only skill one should have mustered and that is the skill to draw. Drawing teaches you to look at anything, be it a creature, a human, a plant or an animal in an entirely different light. Instead of seeing the whole, you learn how to break down your object into shapes and the play of dark and light. Because in a pencil drawing, you cannot identify characteristics using color, you are forced to use shapes, shading and different thickness in lines to create the desired effect. Drawing involves one important tool and that is to be able to see your objects as an assortment of interacting shapes. Therefore, this book takes you through a step-by-step process in creating these bugs by always starting out with identifying a basic recognizable shape.

Finding your own style

Drawing is a creative and meditative diversion. It is important to take time out of the day and just sit and sketch and doodle and hone your drawing skills. Drawing is learned by studying your object with a critical and fresh eye. Drawing is also learned by copying other people's work. I know that tracing or plagiarizing somebodies work is frowned upon, but in the world of drawing it makes a lot of sense, because that is how you learn. Before you can develop your own style, you have to have the skill to put shapes realistically on paper. Trust me when I say this, but the best method ever is to learn from the masters. That is why a step-by-step book is a valuable tool to learn all you need to know about your object you are studying. With time, your own style will emerge on its own. Everybody has a distinctive personality and that characteristics will be reflected in the piece of artwork. So, you will be surprised that as you follow this step-by-step guide, at the end, your drawing will look similar to the one in the book, but your soul will shine through.

A diary with words and images

One of the fun applications of training yourself to sketch and to draw is that you can document the world around you. In the time before cameras, cell phones and technology, scientists relied on their drawing skills to document what they saw. This art form should not be lost in the modern world. I always take a sketchbook on my travels and paint the landscapes, birds and flowers as I see them around me. I add a few words and I love having this collection to reminisce on the places I have been. The art of keeping a visual journal is a fun way to creatively express yourself and have a very personal account of your travels, or studies of nature. How fun would it be to have your own creepy crawler journal with your own observations and thoughts? I think that would be fabulous and by learning about these critters, you are one step closer to your personal study guide. And, hey, how fun could it be to show off your work at the next family function?

That brings me to another thought. What if the next picnic in the park turns a little boring? You can just whip out your sketchbook and your pencil and draw the world around you. It can pass the time and you are creating something lasting and beautiful for yourself and others.

Chapter 2: Tools

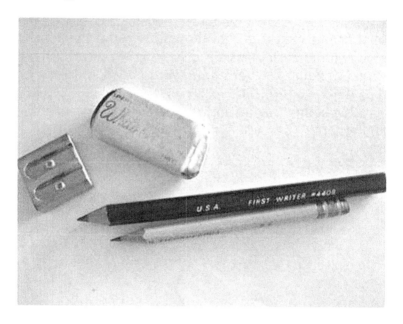

The beauty of drawing is what you need. All you really need just a pencil and a piece of paper. How wonderful is that? I am not a big fan of an eraser, but if you really feel you need one, you should add an eraser to your tool pile. Of course, the pencil needs to stay sharpened, so a pencil sharpener comes in handy as well.

Pencil

The pencil is a valuable component if you want to create your drawings and your shading. To draw your guidelines and your general outlines, a #2 HB pencil is sufficient. I also use it for the hard line shading technique. The beauty in your drawings comes from the play of light and dark. Therefore it is great to have a #6 soft pencil on hand that draws a smooth, delicious line. At the moment, I absolutely love the first writer pencil #4408. It is a little thicker and it shades beautifully and smoothly.

Paper

Smooth drawing paper is better suited then any paper with a rough surface or teeth. Your bright white computer paper will do, but sometimes it is fun to invest in a sketchbook or a pad of Canson drawing paper. But, for sure, you can start this assignment with a piece of paper straight out of your printer.

Pencil sharpener

If you choose the writer's pencil, you will need to purchase a larger holed pencil sharpener. I love the wood version I was able to find at an art store that has a dual function and sharpens a regular pencil along with the fatter one. However, if you stay with regular sized pencil in any lead softness, you can go with a regular school pencil sharpener as well.

Eraser

Okay, as I said, I am not a big fan of erasers. I operate under the conviction that every line that you drew was meant to be there and excessive erasing is stressful and disruptive to the process. Just allow your pencil to flow and know there are no mistakes in art. However, I am using the eraser as tool in our series. For some of the wings, we will employ the eraser to create negative space. I like the white eraser the best, but you may also want to explore the blue kneaded eraser that you can find in any art store.

Storage

You can be as creative as you wish on how you keep your tools together. You can use a pouch, a handy box, or in my case a small ceramic bowl. I like it because it doubles as the trash container for my pencil shavings. Whatever you use, choose something that is compact and easy to store.

Chapter 3: Shapes and shading

As mentioned earlier, it is important to study the shapes of the bug that you are intending to draw. Every object can essentially be broken down into your basic geometric shapes, or at least some versions of it.

The oval

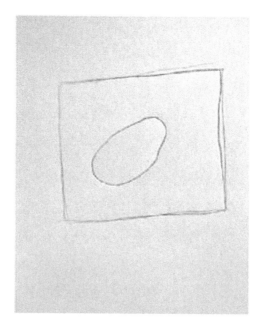

One of the most frequent shapes we come across is the oval. Most bodies of the insects and bugs, heads or tails have a semblance of the oval shape. So, in our process, we typically start out with a line drawing that later on will be shaded to add dimension and definition.

In order to shade our shape, we tilt the pencil slightly on its side and use the broad part of the lead tip to create a fat and smooth texture. Just move the pencil back and forth to create a smooth grey area. To gradate the shading, press a little harder for darker areas and lighter for lighter areas.

Here is a simple example of how your oval should look like while you are in the process of shading. We always create a darker area around the edges and leave a spot in the middle white. That gives the oval dimension and it now looks more like a 3D jellybean. This effect is achieved by varying the shaded areas from dark to light.

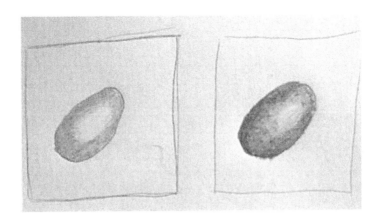

For our final piece, we take the soft lead pencil and add darker spots. Here you can see the gradual transformation of the oval to a jellybean as we add more and more dark shades and gradate the lighter areas with smooth strokes. In order to achieve this, you have to keep drawing over and over your shaded areas. This process is called layering.

The Leg

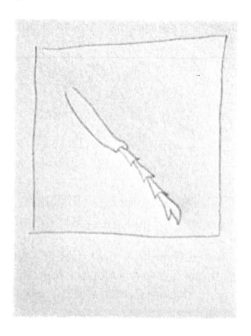

I decided to include a quick study of the multi facetted leg of the insects. Most bugs have a similar version of this limb. Typically, the leg is segmented into three sections. The last part of the leg consists of many little components. In the book I refer to these shapes as interconnecting triangles. At the end of every leg is a little claw. That is mostly used to grab onto leaves or grass stalks or walls. However, what is important in this study is that you focus on the interconnecting triangles and take the time to draw them as such.

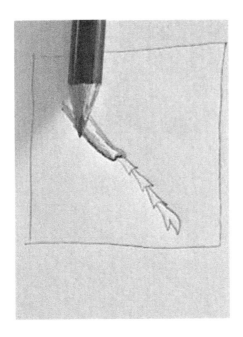

Even though, most of the insect's legs are very skinny, we still want to give them the illusion of a shape, similar to maybe a toothpick or the like. This attention to detail will result in a better, more realistic drawing later on. We use our soft leaded pencil to darken the lines around the leg and shade the inside. Even here, we make sure that the shading softly gradates into a white area. This gives us the illusion of depth and thickness.

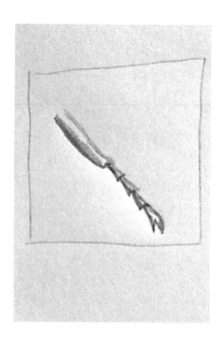

A little care goes a long way. Here you can study a finished segment of the third section of insect legs. As you draw the entire bug, the legs may seem insignificant, but as we pay attention to all the little details, our drawing will look more polished and accomplished.

Chapter 4: Let the Fun Begin

Okay, you are almost ready to dive in, choose your favorite bug and have a go at it. The step-by-step instructions guide you from the beginning outline to the marvelously realistic completion of your bug.

You always want to start out by lightly sketching the outlines. This is really where you hone your observation skills and spend some time staring at the bug. You can track down the real thing or a picture of one and spend some time eyeing all the fascinating details of the body, wings, eyes and legs.

After you have carefully laid down your guidelines and outlines, you can begin to shade and add details to the wings and legs. Maybe a bug is a small creature, but some require quite a lot of time to complete. Perhaps, you want to start out with a less complex crawler like the June bug or the caterpillar, before you tackle the intricate wings of a butterfly, or the hundreds of feet of the centipede. Remember, the devil is in the detail, and you want to spend the time to address every little element.

Caterpillar

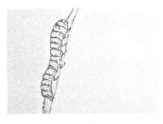

A butterfly egg turns into a caterpillar. Caterpillars have an enormous appetite. They eat and eat and eat themselves through your garden, putting holes into all your green leaves. When it is time for the transformation, the caterpillar will spin a cocoon around itself and wait to emerge as a butterfly. Caterpillars came in many colors and textures. Here we are learning the basic form of this bug.

Step 1.

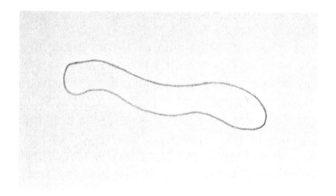

First we want to take a look at the basic shape of the caterpillar. It is basically an elongated oval.

Step 2.

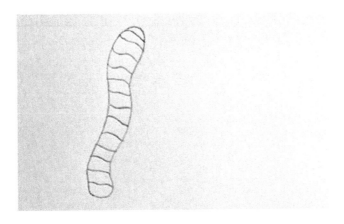

When we take a closer look at the caterpillar, we can see that its body is segmented so it can scoot along the grass stalks. So, our next step is to add the lines to represent the segmentation of the body. These lines need to be drawn with a small curve to show that the body is round.

Step 3.

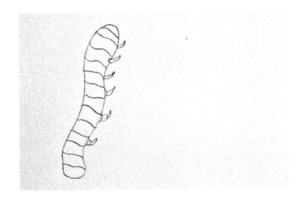

In step 3 we are adding the legs. Typically, the caterpillar has one or two legs in front, around 4 legs in the middle and one towards the end. The legs are rather stubby, so we draw them in a shape of a curved triangle.

Step 4.

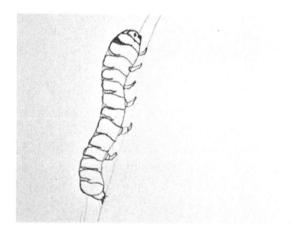

Depending on the butterfly it will turn itself into; the caterpillars have different markings and colors. Our example is the caterpillar that turns into the black swallowtail butterfly. The caterpillar is bright green and has vibrant orange dots on black stripes. As we are creating a black and white pencil drawing, we have to give the illusion of different colors through our shading technique.

In this step, we emphasize and darken our lines that we drew to dissect the body. We are adding squiggly triangles that will be colored black later.

Step 5.

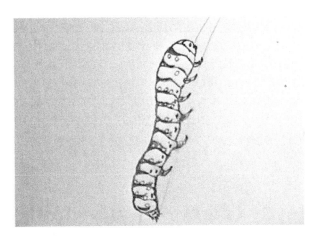

In this step, we continue to develop the body. We add small circles in and around the triangles we just created. After that, we color the triangles black, using our soft lead pencil.

Step 6.

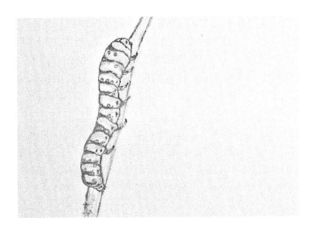

Our last step involves shading the body. We carefully shade each segmented piece at the lines, leaving a white spot in the middle. That way we create the illusion of a rounded bug. We also apply a little shading around the legs. Then we use our soft pencil and darken some of the lines to give some contrast to the drawings. Finally, we pencil in a faint grass stalk to anchor the place the caterpillar occupies in the outside world.

Butterfly (Tiger _Swallowtail)

Well we learned to draw a caterpillar. Now it just makes sense to tackle the transformed caterpillar that is the butterfly. People in general are very fond of this insect. It does not bite, create havoc in the garden or pantry and it looks stunning to boot. To many, the purpose of this insect is to look pretty and delight. However, a butterfly in its winged state also pollinates the flowers and thus helps sustain our flowers and plants.

A butterfly is easy prey, especially when it is in the caterpillar state. It serves as food for many predators. A butterfly's wings are its defense. Sometimes they blend perfectly into the environment, or if it its wings have the bright colors we love so much, it usually signals to the animal kingdom that this animal is dangerous to eat. This allows the butterfly to spend its day happily fluttering from flower to flower and brings joy to all that encounter it.

This butterfly is drawn as a side view. Traditionally, we see a top view, so a side view provides a little more of a challenge.

Step 1.

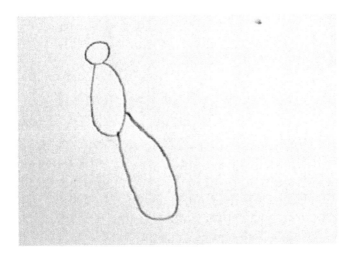

As usual, our first step is to determine the shape of the body for this insect. Even though we will spend the majority of time creating its wonderful wings, it is important to get the body right as well. A butterfly has a small round head, an oval middle body and an oval tail. The middle body and the tail are equal in proportion.

Step 2.

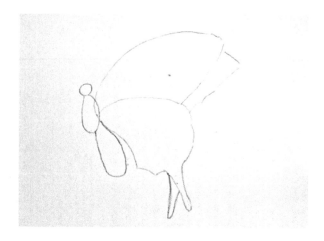

Now we are adding the magnificent wings. Typically, a butterfly has a large set of top wings and a sweeping set of bottom wings. So we just sweep our pencil to create a triangle with rounded sides. We can be very generous with the curves and the size.

Step 3.

Our next step is to add the legs. The butterfly's legs are rather flimsy and not as well muscled as other insects. However, this insect also has a set of three legs on either side of its middle body. They are segmented into three pieces and the last part is also segmented into small triangles. True to all insects, the butterfly has a small claw at the end to grasp onto flowers. Here we also add a contour of the flower to place the butterfly in its environment.

Step 4.

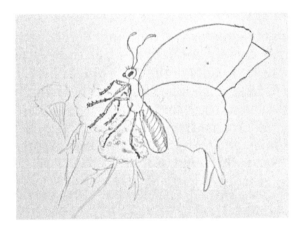

Before we start the hard work on the wings, we concentrate real quickly on shading the legs and the tail. Its tail consists of small segments and we indicate those with slightly curved segment lines. We shade around the lines, making sure that we leave a space of white in the center. Now is the time to add the butterfly's long antlers and a big oval eye.

Step 5.

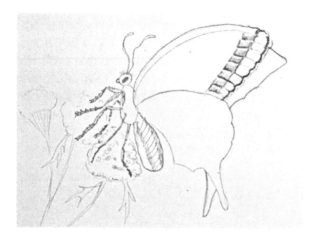

Now we are ready to start the wing. We will go slowly as to capture all the intricacies of the contour lines that create the beauty of the butterfly. Many butterflies have a scalloped edge on the wing. These curves then create the contour lines that we draw into the wind. We repeat those lines and shade the shape that has been created. Basically, we create some sort of band inside the wing.

Step 6.

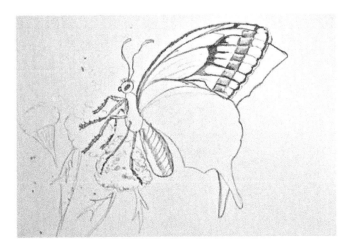

As we are creating this specific type of butterfly, the tiger swallowtail, we follow its wing design. After creating a band, we draw three contour lines to the base of the wing, creating larger shapes. The edging is feathered with black. The main body of this species would be bright yellow.

Step 7.

The largest shape in the wing also is fluted and we again create the look of the band to define the space. The second wing that is showing a little is drawn in a less defined manner, as it is in the background, so it would get more shade from the first wing.

Step 7.

36

The bottom wing is segmented in larger shapes, so we draw less contour lines. Basically, we try to create 5 equal shapes that originated form an almost heart shape space on the wing. The edges are again scalloped, giving the illusion of a folded napkin or fan.

Step 8.

We now draw bands through these 5 shapes. Be careful to flow with the shape of the wing, as you are going up and down like a wave. Shade the bands using varying saturation of the black. For the shading, use your oft pencil. Then go over the wings and darken some lines, creating contest within the wing. A butterfly's body is also slightly firry, so shade the body using quick stroke lines. Finally, we add a little more definition to the flower and here you have your beautiful butterfly.

Monarch Butterfly

Well I am introducing my least favorite bug in these drawing series, so it is just fair that it is time to show off one of my favorite ones as well. The Monarch butterfly is a queen under the beautiful species. It is a wanderer and it is the only insect that is able to cross the Atlantic. It is a migrant. It begins its journey in North America and over winter, it travels to warmer climates. It is able to traverse long distances. Its caterpillar needs milkweed to grow. This herb turns into a toxic substance in the adult butterfly, thus making it lethal to eat by predators. So it is free to roam and be the beautiful wanderer that it is.

Step 1.

First we start of the outline of the body and wings. Of course, a butterfly is all wings and the body is only an elongated oval with a rounded corner for the face. The top wings are a little skewed triangle and the bottom wings are triangles with one side to be curved. Both wings originate for the top half of the body.

Step 2.

The markings of the Monarch butterfly are very distinct. We are going slowly through these steps so the contour lines are carefully followed. In real life, the butterfly is colored orange and black. The contour lines are rather far apart and the lines are thicker and black.

Step 3.

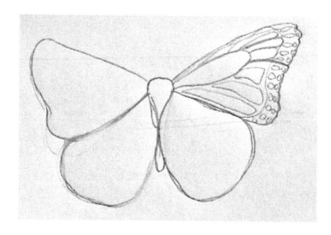

The edge band has small white circles as decorations.

Step 4.

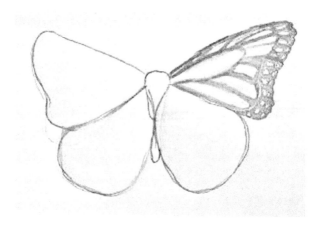

As mentioned before, the dividing contour lines are rather heavy and we are shading them a solid black. We also complete the band on the edge, by carefully filling in the space around the circles. The part that would be orange will be lightly shaded.

Step 5.

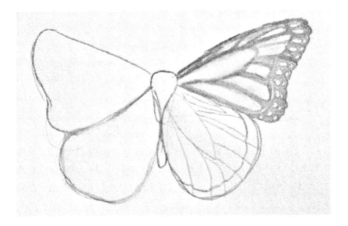

Here we are starting the bottom wing. Again, the contour lines are fatter and the markings are rather bold. The band on the edge continues on the bottom wing as well.

Step 6.

Here we take the time to fill in the bottom wing and darken all the contour lines. The in-between spaces are lightly shaded to show that there may be a color present.

Step 7.

Now it is time to finish the other side just like the first one. It is important to stay as symmetrical as possible, so we take our time to copy one side to the other.

Step 8.

To give the illusion of movement and to emphasize the shimmering wings, we take our eraser and lightly, ever so lightly, rub it over the wings. Light white lines and a few smudges will appear.

Step 9.

Finally we finish the body and the head. We only apply soft shading on these parts and add two eyes in the front of the head. The butterfly also has a set of graceful antennas with a little bubble at the end. Its tail is a little segmented; therefore we add a few contour lines for depth. At the end we take a soft pencil and darken a few lines here and there to create dimension.

Dragonfly

We just tackled one beautiful winged creature, now here is our chance to draw another equally stunning insect. The dragonfly's beauty is in its vibrant colored body paired with long and graceful translucent wings. The dragonfly is also harmless to humans, however it is a predator among the flying insect world. We love her in the garden, as she eats mosquitoes, wasps and flies. So gardeners are delighted when this natural pest controller shows up. Dragonflies love to be near water, so if you live near a steam or have a small pond in the yard, you can hope for some dragonflies as well. They lay their eggs near the water. This insect has a curious nature and it is not afraid of humans. Typically, people also feel joy and delight when happening upon this magnificent insect.

Step 1.

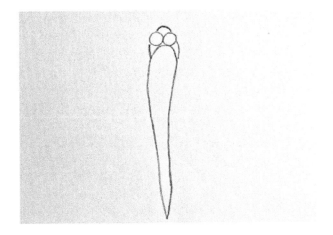

Before we spend most of our time creating the magnificent wings, we also have to lay down the shapes of the body first. A dragonfly's body consists of a long, slender triangle that ends in a tip. Its head is round, however two large, round eyes, dominates it.

Step 2.

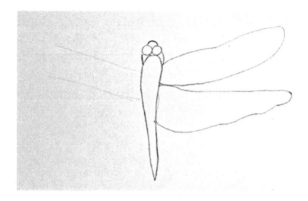

The dragonfly has four wings that ate attached two on each side to its body. The wings are slender and long, in fact some dragonflies can have a wingspan of 3-4inches. The flap their wings very rapidly, so usually you hear some sort of buzzing sound when they come around. The wings are drawn as two stretched out ovals attached to its body. We have to make sure that they are placed within the top half of the body.

Step 3.

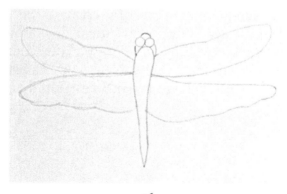

Once we are happy with the wings on one side, we
repeat them on the other side of the body.

Step 4.

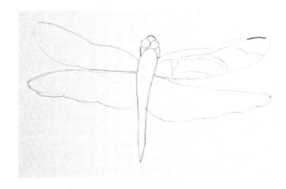

Here we will focus on one wing of the dragonfly. Their
wings have an intricate pattern reminiscent of a
wispy, silky net. First, we lay down the main contour
lines. They basically create 4 or so spaces that we then
fill in.

Step 5.

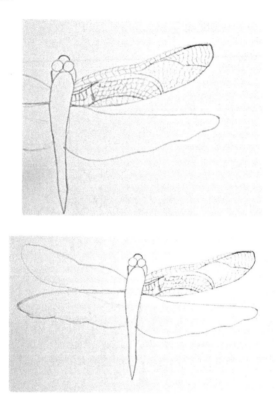

Each space previously created is filled with little
contour lines, forming a small grid. When you place
these lines, think of a delicate translucent web that is
constructed of small little squares. Be sure to follow
your contour lines to create the illusion of the
waviness and organic nature of the wing. This will
take patience and diligence. Really, these wings are
meticulously created one small line at a time.

Step 6.

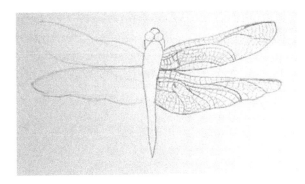

Once we complete the top wing, we start working on the bottom wing. It is created in the same way as we drew the top wing. One small little contour line at a time.

Step 7.

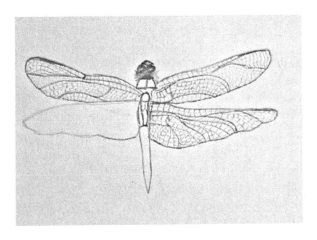

Before we tackle the next wing, let's take a little break and work on the head. The eyes are dominant and large black circles. The head is slightly furry, so we are adding some fuzzy lines around the head. The body is slightly segmented, so we need to add a few contour lines defining the shape of the body. After that, we are back to the wings and just like before, add one contour line after the other until the web is complete.

Step 8.

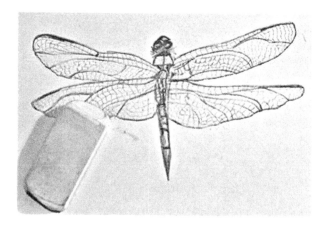

Now all it is left to do is to complete the body and shade in the back half. The body in the drawing appears rather boring, but in reality that is where the dragonfly shines. It comes in brilliant, sparkling and shimmering colors of bright blue, orange or green. Since we are creating a black and white drawing, we are drawing attention to the beauty of its wings. To emphasize the translucent quality, we _ever so slightly-! Rub the eraser over our wing design to blur some of the lines and give the illusion of translucence. Be sure to rub very lightly as not to destroy all the work we have just done.

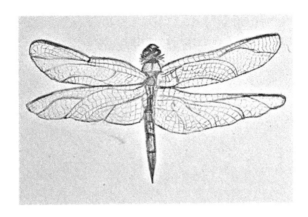

Yeah!

Bee

A bee is a hardworking insect. The expression "busy bee" was inspired by the industrious nature of the beehive. The bees live in a community, where everybody has a purpose. The girls are the worker bees and are busy buzzing around collecting pollen that then is made into honey. When a bee finds a good source of pollen, they tell other bees by the way of a complex dance. Bees are important for those reasons. They provide delicious and nutritious honey and they pollinate our crops, thus ensuring all our fruit and vegetable supply. The bees have one queen that has one purpose. She lays the eggs and when they hatch, the babies are fed with a mixture of pollen and honey. After the baby bees hatch, they become part of the bee community and get their assigned job. Bees have a beautiful way of living and are often misunderstood. They get a bad rep because their sting hurts. However, when they sting you they die, so they are not out to get you. They are just protecting themselves.

Step 1.

Our first step is to outline the shapes of the bee. A bee has a slightly oval head, a round middle body and a larger oval tail. In proportion, the tail is as big as the body and head combined.

Step 2.

Next, we will add the wings. The wings originate in the round middle part of the body. Bee's wings have the shape of a feather and are rather wispy and fragile.

Step 3.

Our third step consists of adding the legs, antennae's and the eye. Like other insects, all 6 legs originate from the middle part of the body, three on each side. The bee also has segmented legs, whereas the last limb is segmented again in small portions. The hind leg of the bee serves as the storage leg for the collected nectar and pollen. Our bee has collected some nectar from the flower, so the second part of her last leg is drawn a little fatter. Her antlers start from the head. We are also adding a simple shape of a flower as to place the bee in its environment.

Step 4.

Now we are working on the details of the body and the legs. As mentioned before, the last segment of the leg is structured in small pieces. For that purpose, we draw little triangles that interconnect and at the end, the bee has a little clay to grasp onto flowers. Her tail is also facetted, so we indicate the different sections with lines. Draw the lines slightly rounded to give emphasis to the curve. In nature, the bee has yellow and black stripes.

Step 5.

Here we add a few more contour lines to the flower. As this is not our main focus, we will keep the flower rather plain. Also, we pay some special attention to the wings. They are translucent and thin, so we apply a slight shade over the wing, making sure that the body underneath still shows. With our soft pencil, we darken some of the wing markings to add contrast.

Step 6.

Our last step includes finishing the shading of the body and legs. A bee is slightly fuzzy, so we apply our shading as small lines around her round middle body, and we add little fur lines to her tail. When we shade the legs, we have to make sure that we always leave a white center, to give the illusion of depth and dimension. Note that we add some pollen to her hind leg.

Moth

A moth is the dark sister of the butterfly. While the beautiful colored butterfly delights during the day, the mysterious moth amazes at night. She is usually colored in earth tones and sporting large eyelike shape in muted hues on her wings. A moth flies by night, but she is attracted to light. Contrary to popular belief, moths do not eat the holes in your wool and linens. In fact, adult moths do not eat at all. They drink the nectar of the flowers. They are essential in pollinating night blooming flowers and artificial light could distract them from their task. The larvae or caterpillar of a moth is a damaging pest, and this is your offender when you see all the holes in your wool coat.

Step 1.

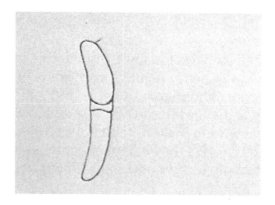

First we study the shapes of the body. A moth is a little heavyset and not as graceful as their sister butterfly. So we draw an elongated, slightly heavier oval for the body of the moth.

Step 2.

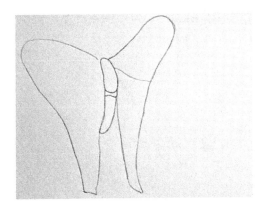

The moth's wings are spectacular. Moths are great fliers and use their antennas to navigate. Here we draw two big sweeping triangles that originate at the top of the body.

Step 3.

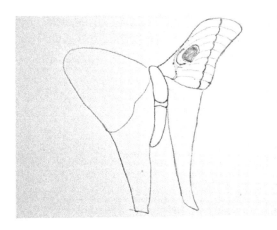

We start focusing on the top right hand wing. First we add the contour lines and a scalloped band along those lines. A slight curved outline emphasizes the drop shaped circle in the wing.

Step 4.

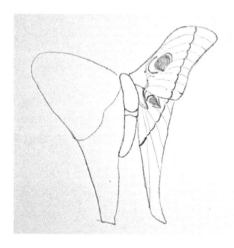

We continue to draw the contour lines into the bottom wing. This moth has sweeping tails on its wing, so the contour band continues fairly high up.

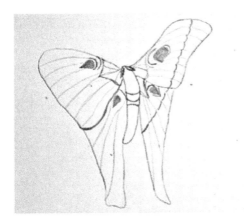

Next we repeat the wing pattern on the other side, trying to keep the symmetry as much as possible. We also add two small fuzzy antennas on the top of her head.

Step 6.

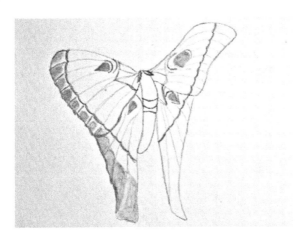

As the moth is fairly monochromatic and her wings are colored in earth tones, we do not create as much contrast as we did before. The wings are carefully and evenly shaded.

Step 7.

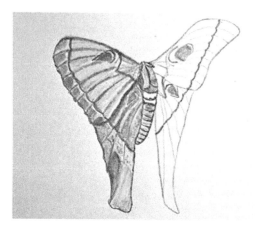

We create some contrast by coloring the drop black and highlighting the contour lines with dark, black lines. All spaces are shaded. The body is slightly segmented and a little hairy, so we add the curved contour lines and a small fuzz to create the hair.

Step 8.

We use the eraser to give the moth a softer look.
Gently wipe the eraser over the wings to smudge some
parts and create soft lines in others.

Step 9.

We finish both sides in equal fashion and notice that the butterfly appears a lot more muted then other insects we drew. We are trying to emphasize its muted and earthy nature.

Chapter 5: Nasty Creatures and Creepy Crawlers

Centipede

If you view this bug as a somewhat creepy crawler, you probably have a point. This bug is technically not an insect, as it has more than 6 legs. However, it does fall short of its thousand legs, it still sports an impressive 30-350 legs depending on its species. Now we are here to illustrate the creature, so we will not attempt to draw 300 legs. We'll keep it around 30. Consequently, this crawler is fast, and can outrun its prey. It eats many bugs, worms and even snails. It is a true predator of the bug world. If you find one, it is good to stay away. It pinches its enemies with its hind legs. Overall, it is a pretty nasty little creature that lives up to a bug's its bad reputation. Its color stays mostly in the brown and the legs are slightly translucent. Our drawing will focus on the many legs and its interesting sectioned body.

Step 1.

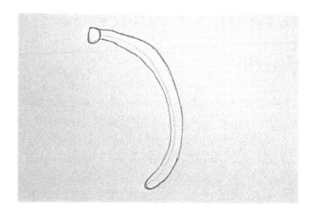

The centipede has a squirmy, wormy body so we try to create a shape that reflects its flexibility. We will draw a wormlike shape with a round circle for its head.

Step 2.

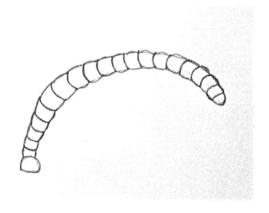

The unique feature of this creature is its flexible body, so we have to segment the worm shape into small spaces. We draw rounded contour lines, equal distance apart along the body. Try to fit at least 15 lines so we can get our leg count in.

Step 3.

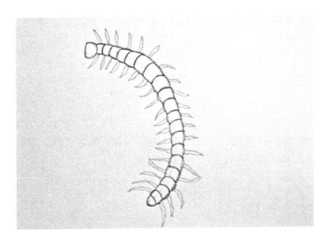

And now it is time to add the legs. Every section will get a pair of legs. The legs are skinny little triangles that are attached to the body. Each consecutive one is a bit larger than the one in front of it. So, yes, the legs are a bit tedious, however they are the defining feature of this bug.

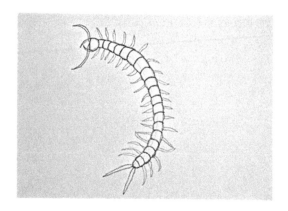

As not to lose sight of these features, here we add two antlers located on the head and two long pincher legs at the tail end of the centipede.

Step 5.

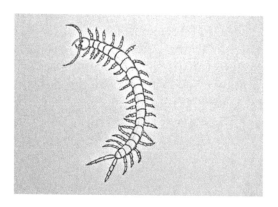

Like many creepy crawlers, the centipede is no exception when it comes to the segmentation of the leg. So here we go back and draw three contour lines in every leg to define the different sections. Don't forget the antennas and pinchers as well.

Lastly, we apply shading to the body and the legs. Here we shade every segment separately and making sure that we leave a white space in the middle. Use your soft pencil to darken some lines to create contrast and definition to the body. And yes, we also have to go back and shade every leg, each segment individually. This will assure us that we capture the organic nature of this bug.

Pincher Bug

As we are on the subject of creepy crawlers, here is by far my least favorite of the bug world. The pincher bug or earwig got his name from the superstition that he crawls into people's ears and bites them. Gross! Even though that is a myth, this bug is a nuisance all on its own. It likes dark, moist places and it goes wherever its hunt for food takes him. He is the scavenger of the lot; he eats all and everything that comes in its way. He eats leaves, foliage, or bugs, dead or alive. Sometimes it also makes its way into your pantry and eats whatever comes to mind in there. It is quite the hunter, scavenger and trash man of the bug world. The fascinating fact about the bug is that it has wings. However it rarely uses them. And the reason why it sports these big pinchers at the end of its tail is that it uses them to open the wings. This seemingly simple bug has quite a complex body make up that has a creepy beauty to it and that is why I included it in our book.

Step 1.

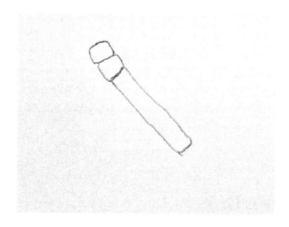

First we need to determine its body shape. It consists of three segments. The head is slightly round, the body is more a rectangle with rounded corners and the tail is the same rectangle but stretched long. Overall, the bug is fairly flat and therefore appears more angular then others in comparison.

Step 2.

Because I like the fact that it has wings, I decided to draw him in this state.

So here we add to wings that are in the shape of a half circle and they are attached to the third segment of its body. It also has to small little rectangular wings that are really the wing covers.

Step 3.

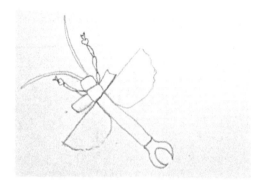

Of course, as a part of the insect family, the pincher bug has 6 legs, three on each side of its body. The legs are segmented into three pieces, and the last one again is divided into many different triangles. St the end of the leg it has small little claws. The pincher bug also has overly long antennas and of course a large claw on its tail.

Step 4.

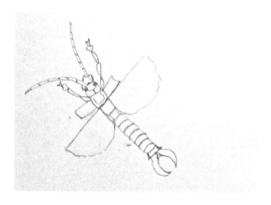

In this step we pay a little more attention to the detail on his body. The head is divided in three and the small eyes are situated towards the front. In addition to the antennas, the pincher bug also has little fangs attached to its head. The tail is segmented into many pieces, allowing for his mobility. We draw the segments as contour lines. Because this bug is rather flat, the contour lines can stay fairly straight. The antlers and the legs are segmented.

Step 5.

The beauty of this bug is his fan shaped wings. They are translucent and were fragile, that is why the shell that needs to be pried open with the claws protects them. We first draw another small half circle within the wing and from that we add contour lines creating a fan like patterns. The edges of the wings are scalloped.

Step 6.

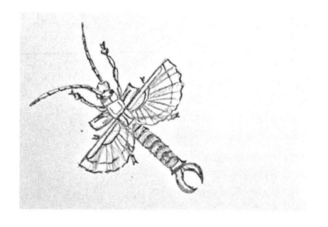

Lastly, we add shading to the wings and the body. The wings are translucent, so we want to add soft lines to the sections and the legs should peek thought faintly. Its body is sleek and black, so we darken his tail and at the end go over the segment lines to create the contrast ewe need. We apply just a little shading to the legs, the head and the pincher claw.

Cockroach

The cockroach also has a first place spot among the creepy bug world. It hides in the shadows and scuttles out at night to do its nasty business. It eats whatever whenever. Nothing is off limits be it your food, other insects or pants. It is like the stinky relative that does not leave and who scarves down all your snacks. It soils all surfaces and food supplies it comes in contact with. It is a dirty bug that spreads disease wherever it steps. They like warm moist places and are found in sewers and wet garbage. Cockroaches have some dubious talents. They can live a long time without water and food. They can hold their breath for 40 minutes and when their head is severed they live on for another week. Overall, this is a nasty bug to have in the house and needs to be cleared out as soon as possible.

Step 1.

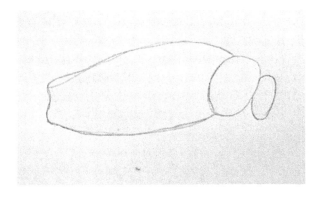

A cockroach has a larger large and flat body. Its head is a flattened oval, the body is round circle and its tail is long and flat.

Step 2.

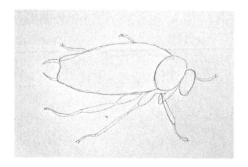

The cockroach also has long, spindly legs. As all insects, it has 6 legs, three on each side of the body. They are segmented into three pieces. The legs of the cockroach are long, but strong. They aid in its ability to scoot through tight spaces and under door slits. At the tail end it has two small pinchers.

Step 3.

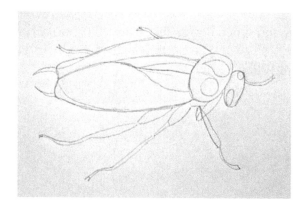

Adult cockroaches can fly and have translucent wings. Here we add the detail to the tail end of the body by showing the wings lying down. The middle part has to teardrop circles and two beady eyes are located in the head.

Step 4.

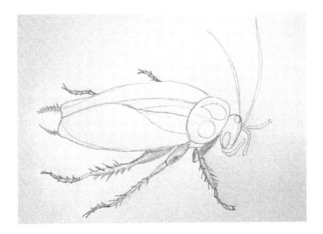

It is time to shade the legs. The cockroach has some hair on its legs. It also sports some large, oversized feelers or antennas. These aid the bug in experiencing the world.

Step 5.

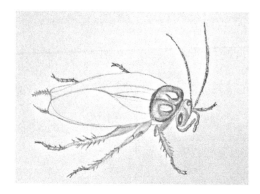

Now we turn our attention to the head and body. A cockroach comes in many colors, but we know it mostly as a brown bug. So we shade the body in a rather uniform manner.

Step 6.

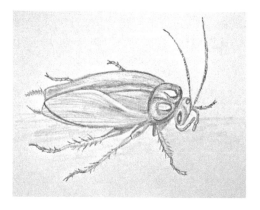

Finally, we add long contour lines to the tail end of the body. The cockroach, despite its flatness has a rather sleek appearance.

Chapter 6: Formidable Predators and Man Eaters

Praying Mantis

This majestic insect is the ultimate predator in the insect world. She is strong, vicious and eats all that come within her path. She bites the neck of her victim to paralyze them and she snacks. A praying mantis can turn their heads 180 degrees and they can see up to 60' far away. The tricky part is that after the praying mantis finds her mate, she bites the head of her mate. Oops. Praying mantis' are not dangerous. In fact, they are beneficial in the yard, as they rid your garden of many pests. They usually live in a forestry area. She received her name because the way she holds her forearms looks like that she is praying. Her body is strong and proud.

Step 1.

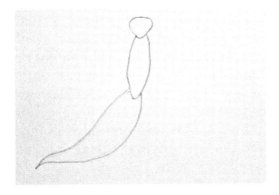

First we are studying the shapes of the body. The praying mantis holds a fairly upright posture, so we draw her head as a tear drop round circle, the she has an oval body and a large tail that ends in a point.

Step 2.

Next we add her legs. The praying mantis also has 6 legs, 3 on each side that originate from the middle body. The unique feature of this insect is that the first set of limbs are powerful and dominant. They are held in what seems to be a praying position, but the praying mantis actually catches her prey with those powerful arms. The last segment has big claws at the end. The rest of the limbs resemble more those of a traditional insect. They are segmented in three sections and the last consists of small triangles that end in a small claw.

Step 3.

A praying mantis also has a set of four wings. They are rather small and have a pointed oval shape. The female insect rarely flies, as her body is so heavy.

Step 6.

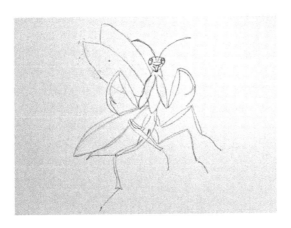

In this step we take a closer look at the face. A praying mantis has two round eyes attached to the side of her head. Its face almost has a resemblance to an alien creature with a nose and a powerful mouth. She also has a set of antennas.

Step 7.

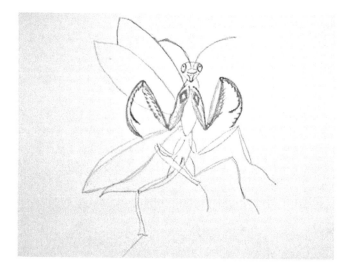

Now it is time to shade the legs. The front legs have a round marking and little spikes. We shade along the outlines, making sure that we leave a white space in the middle to give dimension to the muscles.

Step 8.

Here we continue to shade the rest of the legs.

Step 9.

Her body is a uniform green, so our shading is soft and simple, indicating little contrast. Her tail is segmented, so we add curved contour lines and shade alongside of them.

Step 10.

Her wings bear the markings similar to the dragonfly. They consist of a soft web of squares. Here we pattern the wings into small diamond shapes.

Step 11.

We finish the insect by also completing the bottom wings and at the end; we take our soft dark pencil and darken some of the contour lines.

Scorpion

The scorpion is another creepy crawler that holds a high predatory status. However, it belongs to the spider family with its 8 legs and two claws. A scorpion typically lives in the desert and hides during the day and comes out at night to hunt. It eats all his fellow spiders and insects and his venomous poison sting can be also fatal to humans. However, the scorpion is a shy creature and will not attack people. So scorpion stings remain rare. The scorpion mom carries her babies on her back for quite a long time. It takes them a year to mature. Then it is high time to leave mom,

because she will eat her own when they come near.
Scorpion females are also known to eat their male
companion after mating. Oops. Generally, scorpions
live alone. They do not require a lot of water nor do
they need to eat for a year. That makes them
extremely hardy to survive the harsh desert
environment.

Step 1.

The shape of a scorpion is fairly complex, so we start
the study of its body by drawing guidelines. We try to
get the sweeping tail and the claws in equal
proportion to each other. The scorpion's face is rather
squat.

Step 2.

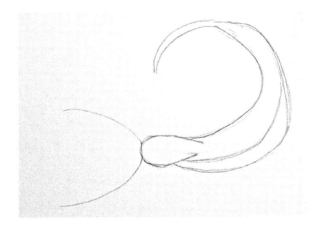

Our next step is to give volume to the tail. The top part is a hard-shelled armor that protects the soft underbelly. The head is integrated into a body and its front is flat.

Step 3.

Next we add the big claws. We can be generous in drawing them, as they are large and dangerous.

Step 4.

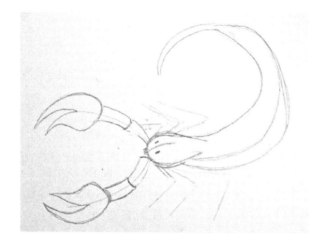

The arms that have the claws attached have segments, so the scorpion can move them freely. So we add the contour lines to show the mobility. We also add guidelines for the rest of the legs that are located close to the top of the body. We also add 2 little beady eyes and a small set of mouth claws.

Step 5.

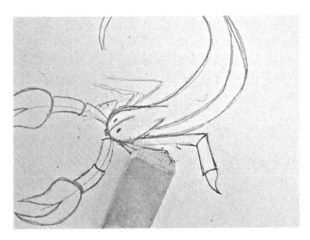

Here we give dimensions to the legs. They are pretty strong and also are segmented in threes. At the end of the leg the scorpion has a little pointer claw. We then carefully erase the guidelines.

Step 6.

Next, we spend some time working on the armor and the shell. The body is sectioned off in many parts that allow the tail end to curve up. So we drew the contour lines in the shape of plates and extend them to the underbelly. Once we arrive at the tail, we will draw ovals that look like a string o beads. At the end, the scorpion carries its formidable stinger.

Step 7.

Now it is time to shade the body. The scorpion is predominantly brown to blend within the sand of the desert. However its body is thick and sculpted, so we shade the edges of the oval shapes, leaving white spots on the middle to create dimension.

Step 8.

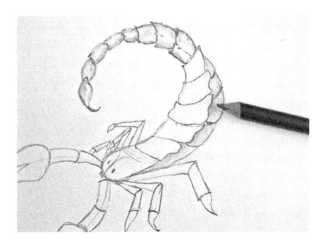

We then shade the underbelly with soft strokes.

Step 9.

In contrast, we apply bolder lines and dots to the armor to give the illusion of the hard shell covering the soft belly.

Step 10.

At the end, we continue to shade the legs and the claws. We locate the scorpion in an environment showing sand and rocks to place him in the desert.

Spider

And here is another wonderful predator that lives a lot closer to the human eye and therefore creates more fear as well as awe in people. However she is a welcome visitor in everybody's garden, as she eats pestering insects. A spider is a vicious predator of the bug world. She spins an absolutely beautiful web to catch unsuspecting pray with it. Once caught, the struggling insect only gets itself more and more tangled until it succumbs to the spider's venomous bite. The spider is the artist among the creepy crawler. If you ever have a chance, study a freshly spun spider web and marvel at its symmetry and beauty. Female spiders also eat their male companions after mating. It seems it is just not a good idea to be a partner of these predatory females. Certain spider bites may also be harmful to humans, so caution is prudent around this species. A spider, unlike an insect has 8 legs, while the bugs typically have 6 legs.

Step 1.

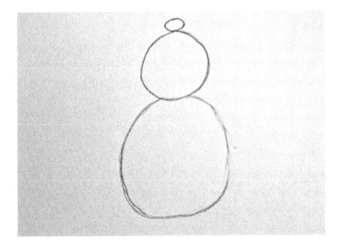

First we study the shape of the spider's body. Typically, a spider is rather round, so draw three circles. The first small circle represent its pinchers in front, the next larger circle is its body and the largest one its tail.

Step 2.

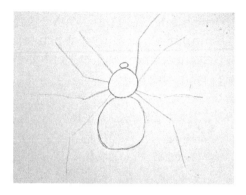

We also first draw guidelines for the 8 legs, 4 on each side. All the legs originate from the middle circle, the body part. The legs are the identifying element of the spider. They are long, hairy and strong.

Step 3.

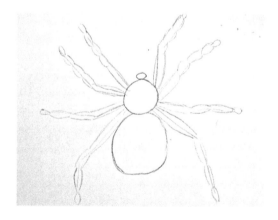

As with an insect, the legs of the spider are also segmented for mobility. Here we give dimension to the legs and add the contour lines to show the different sections.

Step 4.

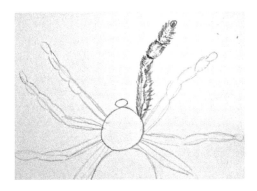

Now it is time to shade the leg. Our example has very hairy fat legs, so we shade it by using quick dark strokes. Make sure to leave white space in the middle to give dimension to the limb.

Step 5.

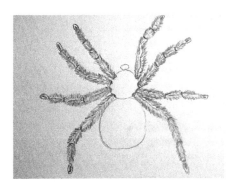

We continue with shading all the spiders 8 legs.

Step 6

Lastly, we finish the body. It is equally hairy and our example has a marking on her back. We define the pinchers in front and shade in the eyes.

Wasp

A wasp is like the angry, mean sister of a bee. Whereas we tolerate bees and love them for their honey, we have no appreciation for the wasps. Even though they also fall in the category of the predatory insects, we are hard pressed to thank the wasp for killing flies, when they swarm our picnic food and sting us. Wasps unlike the bees do not die when they use their stinger, but they use them repeatedly and they bite. Ouch! The question occurs, do I tolerate the pesky flies, or do aggressive wasps sting me? Because, if they feel threatened, they will attack. If you happened to get stung by a wasp, she releases a scent that alerts other wasps to come to her defense. Hmm, that does not sound like fun. Especially if you come across a hornet that is a large version of a wasp. Wasps built fascinating nests out of paper and clay. They produce the paper by chewing wood and plant materials and built them in beautiful nests. They live in organized colonies, similar to the bees. As mentioned before, they are predators and eat themselves around the insect world. Their striking black and yellow coloring warns anybody that this is a bug not to be messed with.

Step 1.

First we lay down the body shapes for the wasp. She looks very similar to the bee, but is sleeker and more streamlined and not as fuzzy. The head is a skewed oval, followed by an oval shaped body and another oval shaped tail that ends in a point. In proportion, the tail is in equal proportion to the body and head.

Step 2.

The wasps' wings are thin and skinny. We just draw them as an elongated, thin oval that originates from the center of the body.

Step 3.

The wasp has 6 legs, three on each side of the body as well. The legs are segmented. Wasps like to eat sweets, so to place her in her environment, we add a round beery to the drawing.

Step 4.

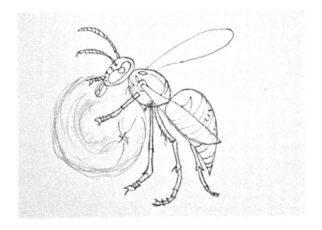

Now it is time to add detail to the legs and the body. The legs consist of three segments and the last piece consists of many small triangles. At the end, the wasp has a small little claw. The tail is also segmented and is colored in black and yellow stripes. A wasp has a big, a little angry looking eye that we place on the head. She also has two antennas and protruding pinchers at her mouth.

Step 5.

Now it is time to pay attention to the wings. They have few contour lines and are translucent. Therefore we have to make sure that the body shows through.

Step 6.

At last, we shade the insect. We apply simple strokes to the wings to show their filmy nature. We make sure that we highlight the markings of the tail. The legs are simply shaded and we give the round fruit some dimension along the circular line. We add a faint outline of grass stalks to place the wasp within its environment.

Chapter 7: Pesky Pests and Annoying Critters

Ant

There are many different kinds of ants, but today, we are focusing on the basic house ant that sometimes finds its way into your pantry. Unfortunately, it does not come by itself, but brings thousands of friends along. Ants have very sensitive antlers that can smell where food is to be found. Ants live in colonies where they have special jobs. Some built the mound, some search for food and some protect the queen. Ants are very hard workers and seldom take a break.

Step 1.

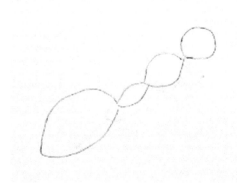

Our first step is to lay down the basic shape of the ant. An ant has a limber body. It is arranged in shapes that allow the ant to move over obstacles. So first we draw a circle for the head, then a medium oval for the first part of the body, followed by a small oval and a large end piece. In proportion, the last end piece should be about the same size as the two ovals in front of it.

Step 2.

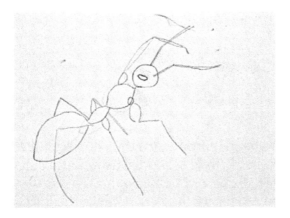

Now we are adding the legs and antlers. In this step, we are drawing just the guidelines that we later fill in. The first set of legs start at the first body oval and the two other sets are located in the second body oval. Each leg is arranged in sections. First you draw a little circle, followed by an oval then three leg parts. The last section consists of multiple limbs.

The antlers protrude from the head. The ant also has a big eye on the side of its face.

Step 3.

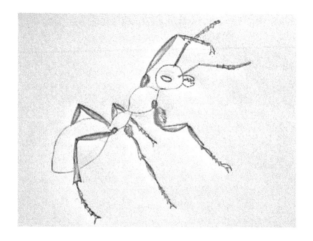

Next, we spend a little more time developing the legs. The first small circle is shaded around the edges, so it creates the illusion of being round. The next oval has some hair, so we use lines to achieve the look of hair. Then we create the segments to the legs, paying close attention to the last limb that is segmented in small little triangle parts. At the end the ant has a little claw shape. The antlers are also segmented.

Step 4.

For our last step, we need to shade the body. The head and the two first small oval shapes are just simple round forms that can be shaded to give the illusion of a body. The tail has a few separation lines. They need to be drawn with the curve of the body and each segment is shaded separate. That helps to round the tail and create movement within the animal. Last we add just a few lines and dots to create the ground.

Mosquito

Oh the pesky mosquito, we all had an experience with their itchy bites. But, in fact, only the mosquito girls squeak around you at night or at the campsite and land on you to bite you and suck out your blood. Yuck! But she needs this nourishment to hatch her babies. When you come upon a mosquito swarm, most likely you will find all the boys gathered in there. They all wait for one girl to show up, they mate, and then the girl is on the hunt for you, the human to get some blood to hatch her eggs. She has three days to do so. Mosquitoes flog to the light, so oftentimes it is a mistake to leave your window open at night when the light is on. Mosquitoes breed in stagnant water, so it is also important to not be close to stagnant water sources like a pond. Overall, the mosquito is a human nuisance, but the frog enjoys the squeaking insect. The one actually should call it a high pitch whine is really the mosquitoes love song to attract their partner. Okay, yeah, but not at night please!

Step 1.

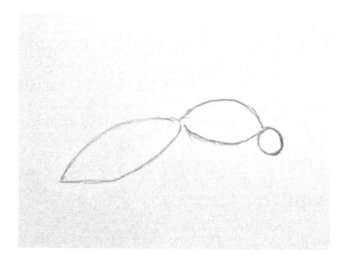

First, we study the mosquito's body shape. The mosquito is actually a pretty awkward character. Its body is slightly bent. So its head and its body need to be drawn in a slight bend. The tail is a slender oval that in proportion is the same as the two other parts combined.

Step 2.

The wings originate from the top of its body part. They are pointed at the entry and stretch out into a long oval. The mosquito's wings are skinny and not very impressive.

Step 3.

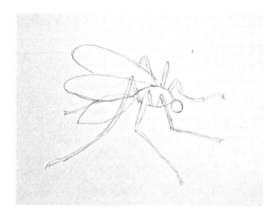

Now we are concentrating on the leg. The mosquito has long, gangly legs in proportion to its body. So it is okay to really stretch those segments, especially the hind legs. All 6 legs originate from the middle body, three on each side.

Step 4.

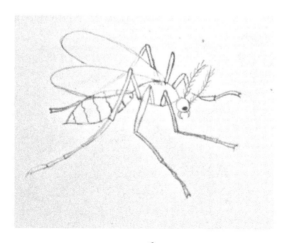

Here we are focusing on the detail on the body and the legs. A mosquito has a set of fuzzy antennas that look like branches of a fir tree. The legs are segmented, however every species is longish, compared to the other insects. The tail is also portioned of and we indicate this by drawing slightly curved and slightly wavy lines. The mosquito has two sharp fangs in the front of its head and two small black round eyes.

Step 5.

The wings, as mentioned, are ordinary. We are just adding a few long and basic contour lines to our shapes and slightly shade the space in-between.

Step 6.

To finish up our squeaky mosquito, we add texture and shading to the body and legs. The body part is slightly fuzzy, so we use quick little strokes to create the fur. The legs are shaded on one side, leaving a little white to create dimension. At the end, we use our black soft pencil to darken some of the lines.

Snail

A snail is a very common bug, if that is what we can call it. It belongs to the mollusk family due to the shell on its back and its one foot. A snail lives about anywhere and mostly comes out at night and in the early morning to feed on your garden. It is a much-despised pest, and it ruins many vegetables and flowers. IA snail scoots along on by expanding and contracting its one foot. It leaves behind a trail of slime, which makes the movement easier. Snails have a beautiful shell on their backs that offers an instant house to sleep in and some form of protection from predators. They cannot hear, so they rely on their sensitive antennas to explore their environment.

Step 1.

A snail has a rather simple shape. The body consists of one long oval and the shell is drawn as a round circle on its back.

Step 2.

The snail has feelers that protrude from its head. We draw them as a sort of branch sticking out of the fort of the head.

Step 3.

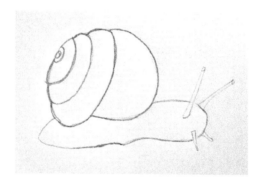

The shell is configured in some sort of spiral. It is said that the snail adds a spiral every year of its life.

Step 4.

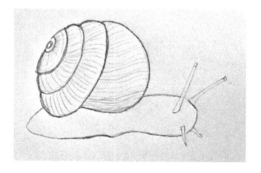

Now it is time to give definition and decoration to the snails' shell. They are usually brown in color but have beautiful markings and a graceful subtle design. So we add thin contour lines to emphasize the round nature of the shell.

STEP 5.

The body of the snail looks like a wrinkly finger. The underside contains a powerful, segmented muscle that scoots the snail forward and the soft body goes along with the motion. A snail really is a very crinkled and slimy affair. Yuck!

Step 6.

At the end, we shade the body lightly, making sure that the wrinkle lines as well as the shell lines show through.

Fly

This insect is a pesky pest. They smell their food and their taste buds are 100 times more sensitive in comparison to humans. Flies can only eat liquids and they suck on the food like a vacuum cleaner. They are able to turn most solid foods into liquid by vomiting on it. They also lay their eggs onto our fare and out come the maggots. Yuck! Flies are pests to humans and carry diseases. They spoil food and pretty much are a nuisance all the way around. Their one distinguishing feature is their unique, multifaceted eyes. They see the world very different then us.

Step 1.

A fly has an oval shaped body. The head is dominated by its large round eyes, the body is rather round and the tail is an oval that has a slight point at the end.

Step 2.

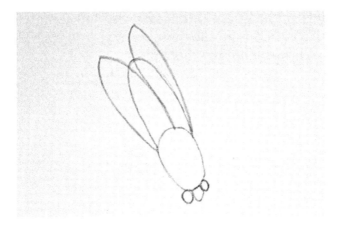

A fly has skinny nondescript wings that originate at the base of its round body. The wings are oval shaped with a point at the end.

Step 3.

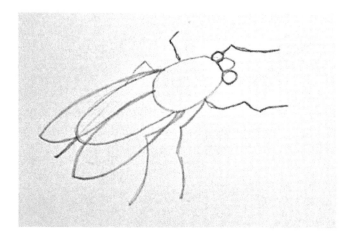

The legs of the fly are rather scrawny and skinny. All 6 legs originated from the middle body, 3 on each side. They are segmented in three pieces.

Step 4.

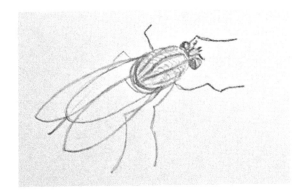

Here we spend some time shading the fly's body. A fly has sparse hair and its body is black. Some flies have a green shimmer to its facets on the surface. The eyes are large and dark; In addition, the fly has small little pinchers at its mouth, as well as tiny little hairy antennas.

Step 5.

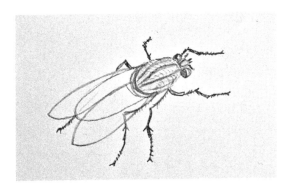

As described before, the legs are skinny and scrawny, so we draw them with thin dark lines. The legs also have sparse hair. The last segment of the limb is divided in small triangles for mobility and at the end of the leg it has a little claw.

Step 6.

The rest of the body, including the tail is very plain. It is also black, shows some feint contour lines and sparse hair.

Step 7.

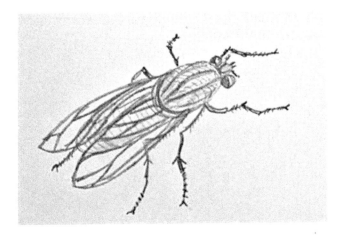

The wing structure is simple and consists of a few contour lines. The wings are translucent, so we have to make sure the body shows though underneath.

Step 8.

Here we shade the wings lightly and then use the eraser to smudge the lines and add some small white splotches. This gives the illusion of the translucence and organic nature of the leaves.

Step 9.

At the end, we take pour soft pencil and add some black lines here and there to create depth.

Chapter 8: Happy Buggers

June Bug

This bug got his name from the fact that they appear in large numbers just at the beginning of June. Large swarms will descend on the farms and gardens and they buzz around, announcing the beginning of summer. They are intensely attracted to light, so if you have your lamp on an early June night you are sure to have a jittering June bug flitting around in your room. June bugs are the harbingers of summer and therefore well tolerated. However, they are a danger to crops and leaves, as they are vegetarian in nature. The larva develops underground and it can stay there as long as three years before hatching. In that time, it can do a lot of damage to roots of which they feed. Wild pigs, skunks and birds root the larvae of the June bug.

Step 1.

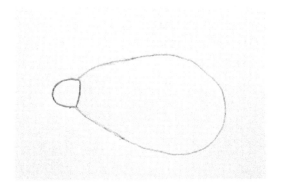

First we study the shape of the bug. Bugs are somewhat easy to draw, as they consist of a small head and a large oval body.

STEP 2.

The June bug also has 6 legs, 3 on each side of its body. As we learned from the very beginning, the legs are segmented into three pieces. Right now, we are just drawing some guidelines to help us establish the location and nature of the legs. The June bug also has to big round eyes, small antennas, pinchers and little fan antennas. I chose this species of the June bug, because I like his fan antennas. It makes him more interesting to draw. Not all June bugs have those.

Step 3.

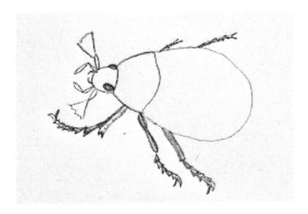

Here we develop the legs. The first and second segments are smooth and the third is divided into small triangles that end in a small claw.

Step 4.

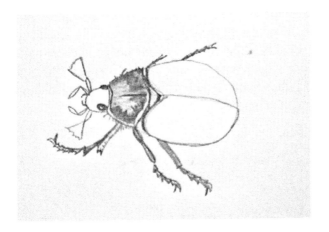

Now we are working a little more on its body. Its middle part is black and slightly fuzzy. So we need to shade this part rather dark and add lines to represent the fuzz.

Step 5.

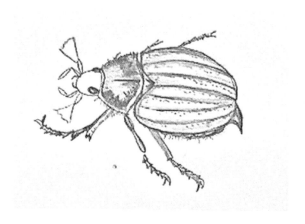

The last part of his body represents the shell that hides and protects the fragile wings. The shell has long contour lines and is rather hard. We draw the lines in a slight curve to give definition to the body. We add a little bit of stopple to show that the shell is tough and a little rough.

Step 6.

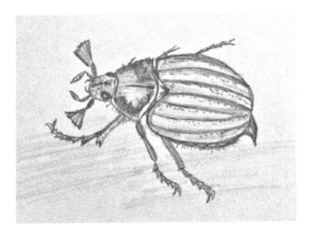

Lastly, we finish shading the head and the fan like antennas to complete the bug. With our soft pencil, we darken some of the lines to add contrast and define the shapes.

Lady Bug

A ladybug is a welcomed visitor in everyone's garden. They feed mostly of plant lice and therefore are even known to be placed in a garden to rid the plants and flowers of this pest. Lady Bugs warn away many predators with their bright red color. Indeed, they taste absolutely bitter and nasty to many birds and other insects that most leave them alone. When threatened they squeezed a yellow fluid out of their legs that is bitter and sharp smelling and tasting. The fun dots are just a marking and do not indicate their age. A ladybug is considered to be a happy bug and is a well-received lucky bug to have around the garden.

Even though, this bug is technically a beetle, but who is looking?

Step 1.

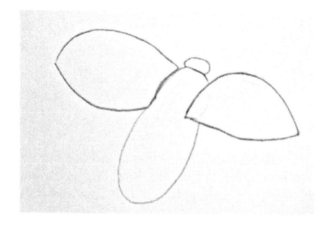

We first need to lay down the general shape of the body. Because I chose to highlight the unique look of the ladybugs wings, we are drawing the beetle in flight. It has a small round head, and a long oval body. The wing covers are two half circles that are attached to the body, towards the front.

Step 2.

The fragile wings feather out from under the wing
cover. We will draw them like a fan with soft scalloped
edges. The ladybug also has 6 legs, however from our
perspective, only the front and hind legs will show. So
here we give the indication of front legs peeking out
behind his wing cover.

Step 3.

Now it is time to add the hind legs. They are segmented into three and spread a little away from his body when he is in flight. The ladybug also has small antennas and round little eyes that are located towards the side.

Step 4.

Now it is time to add detail to the body in the wing covers. Of course, this is a ladybug, so we add round circles to the wing cover that will represent the black dots. The last half of its body is segmented. We add slightly curved contour lines to give the impression of a rounded body. The legs are slightly fuzzy and the last third is segmented as well. We indicate this by drawing a few small triangles that are interconnected. At the end of each foot will be a claw.

Step 5.

Now we turn our attention to the wings. These wings are translucent and fragile, a little like a sheer curtain. We darken the contour lines and shade the wings in soft lines. The body should peek through the wings to indicate that they are indeed see-through.

Step 6.

Our last step involves shading all the parts of its body. The wing cover is slightly curved, so we apply a little deeper shading on top and graduate it down in soft curves. The legs are shaded on one side, leaving white exposed to create depth. The body of the ladybug is black. We use our soft pencil to darken the body and draw over the contour lines to create depth!

Grasshopper

The grasshopper is probably one of the more romantic insects. The male rubs his legs together to create a song that attracts the female. And you may notice that the female grasshopper does not eat her mate. He is definitely doing something right. As humans, we love to sit outside on a warm summer night and listen to the chirping song of a grasshopper. It is meditative and soothing. However, if you are a farmer, you may think differently. Grasshoppers are known to swarm over fields and eradicate the entire crop over night. They eat leaves in all varieties, but the softer the better. Aside from playing their romantic melodies at night, they also have a great hop. Thanks to their strong hind legs, they are able to jump up to 20 times higher than their body length. That would be a cool thing to do.

Step 1.

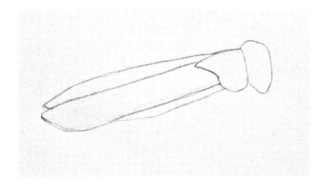

The body of a grasshopper is long and streamlined. It has a slightly oval head and long streamlined wings that are attached to a little collar around the head.

Step 2.

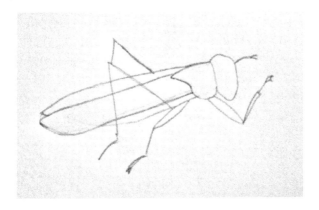

The legs are an important feature of the grasshopper. Its hind legs are well developed, because he uses those to jump. Here we lay down the guidelines for the 6 legs, 3 on each side of the body. Again, special attention needs to be paid to the larger and stronger hind legs.

Step 3.

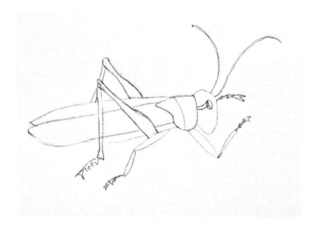

Now it is time to fatten up the lines and give dimension to the limbs. The legs are strong and sectioned off. The last piece is segmented into small triangles that end into a claw. The grasshopper also has two long antennas. He has a small eye and a curious, alien like face.

Step 4.

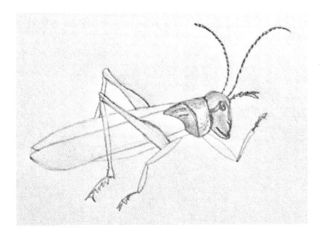

Here we start to shade the head and the collar. A grasshopper has a hard shell, so we use lines and stipples to show the hard armor.

Step 5.

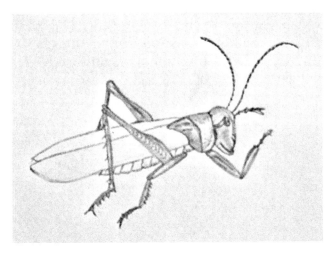

The legs are shaded around the lines. We need to leave a white space in the middle to give the illusion of depth. The first segment of the hind leg has a special herringbone pattern.

Step 6.

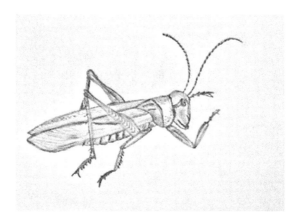

The wings are simple and have thin contour lines that follow the shape and outline of the wing. The wings are translucent, so we shade them softly. The body is facetted and we add the slightly curved lines to show the rounded belly. A grasshopper is uniformly green colored without a lot of contrast.

Step 7.

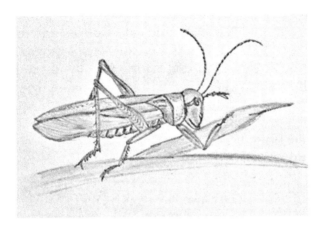

For the final picture, we add some grass to place him into the environment that he belongs to.

About the Expert

Stefani Neumann is born and raised in a small town in Germany and has spent many hours exploring the outdoors. She also studied design and spent even more hours learning how to draw and paint. Today, she combines her talents by teaching art in an outreach program to young and old. In fact, she has been teaching drawing for over 10 years and enjoys every minute of it.

HowExpert publishes quick 'how to' guides on all topics from A to Z by everyday experts. Visit HowExpert.com to learn more.

Recommended Resources

- HowExpert.com – Quick 'How To' Guides on All Topics from A to Z by Everyday Experts.
- HowExpert.com/free – Free HowExpert Email Newsletter.
- HowExpert.com/books – HowExpert Books
- HowExpert.com/courses – HowExpert Courses
- HowExpert.com/clothing – HowExpert Clothing
- HowExpert.com/membership – HowExpert Membership Site
- HowExpert.com/affiliates – HowExpert Affiliate Program
- HowExpert.com/writers – Write About Your #1 Passion/Knowledge/Expertise & Become a HowExpert Author.
- HowExpert.com/resources – Additional HowExpert Recommended Resources
- YouTube.com/HowExpert – Subscribe to HowExpert YouTube.
- Instagram.com/HowExpert – Follow HowExpert on Instagram.
- Facebook.com/HowExpert – Follow HowExpert on Facebook.

Printed in Great Britain
by Amazon